Spiritual
GROWTH PLAN

PASTOR TYRONE LUINES

Spiritual
GROWTH PLAN

Preparing for an Abundant Harvest

XULON PRESS

Xulon Press
2301 Lucien Way #415
Maitland, FL 32751
407.339.4217
www.xulonpress.com

© 2021 by Pastor Tyrone Luines

All rights reserved solely by the author. The author guarantees all contents are original and do not infringe upon the legal rights of any other person or work. No part of this book may be reproduced in any form without the permission of the author. The views expressed in this book are not necessarily those of the publisher.

Due to the changing nature of the Internet, if there are any web addresses, links, or URLs included in this manuscript, these may have been altered and may no longer be accessible. The views and opinions shared in this book belong solely to the author and do not necessarily reflect those of the publisher. The publisher therefore disclaims responsibility for the views or opinions expressed within the work.

Unless otherwise indicated, Scripture quotations taken from the King James Version (KJV) – *public domain.*

Scripture quotations taken from the Holy Bible, New International Version (NIV). Copyright © 1973, 1978, 1984, 2011 by Biblica, Inc.™. Used by permission. All rights reserved.

Scripture quotations taken from the Amplified Bible (AMP). Copyright © 1954, 1958, 1962, 1964, 1965, 1987 by The Lockman Foundation. Used by permission. All rights reserved.

Scripture quotations taken from the New King James Version (NKJV). Copyright © 1982 by Thomas Nelson, Inc. Used by permission. All rights reserved.

Paperback ISBN-13: 978-1-6628-3233-8
eBook ISBN-13: 978-1-6628-3234-5

SPIRITUAL GROWTH PLAN

Name: _____

Season: _____

Date: _____

SPIRITUAL GROWTH IS IMPORTANT (2 Peter 3:18 & 1 Timothy 4:15)! Anything that is important is worth being intentional about accomplishing (Luke 14:28 & Habakkuk 2:2). Just like farming, you cannot force spiritual growth but you can be intentional about making the conditions right for God to yield an increase in your life (Psalm 92:13 & I Corinthians 3:6-9). It is both the responsibility of the individual believer and church leadership (specifically the pastor-teacher) to make conditions right for spiritual growth (1 Peter 2:2 & 5:2). Therefore, we encourage pastors and/or leaders to meet with every member four times a year (every season) to develop, discuss and assess spiritual growth (membership has its privileges).

Attached you will find an evaluation which identifies the following five areas of spiritual life that can be used to evaluate spiritual growth. The five things you need to succeed are Self-denial, Cross-bearing, Abiding, Gift Sharing and Transformation.

The individual church member will, in writing, express their goals and plans to accomplish those goals in each of the five areas. After submitting these goals to their pastor/leader, they, along with their pastor/leader will evaluate the appropriateness and requirements of each goal and plan. After prayer and execution, a time will be arranged to evaluate and modify, as necessary, each goal and the plan associated with that goal. The overall goal of spiritual growth being maturity.

May God bless all of our endeavors to establish and expand His Kingdom in arranging our lives in accordance with His revealed will. In Jesus' Name!

Tyrone Luines
Senior Pastor, Croft Christian Church

TABLE OF CONTENTS

Introduction 1

I. Self-Denial **3**
Acknowledging God 5
Repentance 7
Overcoming Temptation 9
Praise in the Midst of Problems 13

II. Cross Bearing **16**
Service 18
Obedience 20
Perseverance 22
Peacemaking 25

III. Abiding **28**
Scripture Memorization 30
Daily Devotion 32
Attitude of Gratitude 35
Local Church Participation 37

IV. Gift Sharing **40**
Sharing Spiritual Gifts 42
Taking Advantage of Witnessing Opportunities 44
Giving Time, Talents and Treasure to God 46
Showing Compassion 48

V. Transformation **50**
Filled and Lead by The Spirit 52
Showing Love: Edifying, Encouraging Thoughts, Words and Deeds- Self and Others. 55
Engage in Opportunities to Nurture Someone's Spiritual Growth 58
Turning Negatives Into Positives 60
Conclusion 63

SPIRITUAL GROWTH PLAN

I. Self-denial (Mark 10:28)

Matthew 16:24 *Then said Jesus unto his disciples, If any man will come after me, let him **deny himself**, and take up his cross, and follow me.*

Acknowledging God
*Proverbs 3:6 In all thy ways **acknowledge** him, and he shall direct thy paths.*

Goal:

Current Rating: 0-5 (5 being the highest)   0   1   2   3   4   5

Plan:

Repentance
*Hebrews 6:1 Therefore leaving the principles of the doctrine of Christ, let us go on unto perfection; not laying again the foundation of **repentance from dead works**, and of faith toward God,*

Goal:

Current Rating: 0-5 (5 being the highest)   0   1   2   3   4   5

Plan:

Overcoming Temptation
*Hebrews 12:1 Wherefore seeing we also are compassed about with so great a cloud of witnesses, let us **lay aside every weight, and** the **sin** which doth so easily **beset us**, and let us run with patience the race that is set before us,*

Goal:

Current Rating: 0-5 (5 being the highest) 0 1 2 3 4 5

Plan:

Praise in the midst of problems
1 Peter 1:6 *Wherein ye greatly **rejoice**, **though now** for a season, if need be, ye are **in heaviness** through manifold temptations:*

Goal:

Current Rating: 0-5 (5 being the highest) 0 1 2 3 4 5

Plan:

II. Cross bearing (Matthew 10:38)

Luke 9:23 *And he said to them all, If any man will come after me, let him deny himself, and **take up his cross daily**, and follow me.*

Service
Mark 10:45 *For even the Son of man came not to be ministered unto, but to minister, and to give his life a ransom for many.*

Goal:

Current Rating: 0-5 (5 being the highest) 0 1 2 3 4 5

Plan:

Obedience
John 14:15 *If ye love me, keep my commandments.*

Goal:

Current Rating: 0-5 (5 being the highest)   0   1   2   3   4   5

Plan:

Perseverance
Luke 22:42 (KJV) Saying, Father, if thou be willing, remove this cup from me: nevertheless not my will, but thine, be done.

Goal:

Current Rating: 0-5 (5 being the highest)   0   1   2   3   4   5

Plan:

Peacemaking
*Matthew 5:9 Blessed are the **peacemakers**: for they shall be called the children of God.*

Goal:

Current Rating: 0-5 (5 being the highest)   0   1   2   3   4   5

Plan:

III. Abiding (1 John 2:28)

*John 15:4 **Abide** in me, and I in you. As the branch cannot bear fruit of itself, except it **abide** in the vine; no more can ye, except ye **abide** in me.*

Scripture Memorization (Ps 119:11)
*Joshua 1:8 This book of the law shall not depart out of thy mouth; but thou shalt **meditate** therein **day and night**, that thou mayest **observe to do** according to **all** that is written therein: for then thou shalt make thy way **prosperous**, and then thou shalt have **good success**.*

Goal:

Current Rating: 0-5 (5 being the highest)   0   1   2   3   4   5

Plan:

Daily Devotion (Planned Prayer Time & Intensity)
Colossians 4:2 Continue in prayer, and watch in the same with thanksgiving;

Goal:

Current Rating: 0-5 (5 being the highest)   0   1   2   3   4   5

Plan:

Attitude of gratitude-
(Philippians 4:4-9) esp. *v8 Finally, brethren, whatsoever things are **true**, whatsoever things are **honest**, whatsoever things are **just**, whatsoever things are **pure**, whatsoever things are **lovely**, whatsoever things are of **good report**; if there be any **virtue**, and if there be any **praise**, **think on these things**.*

Goal:

Current Rating: 0-5 (5 being the highest)   0   1   2   3   4   5

Plan:

Local church participation
*Hebrews 10:25 Not forsaking the **assembling of ourselves together**, as the manner of some is; but exhorting one another: and so much the more, as ye see the day approaching.*

Goal:

Current Rating: 0-5 (5 being the highest)   0   1   2   3   4   5

Plan:

IV. Gift Sharing (Ephesians 4:16)

Philippians 2:4 Look not every man on his own things, but every man also on the things of others.

Sharing spiritual gifts
Romans 12: 6 *Having then **gifts differing** according to the grace that is given to us, whether prophecy, **let us** prophesy **according to the proportion of faith**;*

Goal:

Current Rating: 1-5 (5 being the highest)   0   1   2   3   4   5

Plan:

Taking advantage of witnessing opportunities
Acts 1:8 *But ye shall receive power, after that the Holy Ghost is come upon you: and **ye shall be witnesses** unto me both in Jerusalem, and in all Judaea, and in Samaria, and unto the uttermost part of the earth.*

Goal:

Current Rating: 1-5 (5 being the highest)   0   1   2   3   4   5

Plan:

Giving of time, treasure and talent
2 Corinthians 9:7 *Every man according as he purposeth in his heart, so let him give; not grudgingly, or of necessity: for God loveth a cheerful giver.*

Goal:

Current Rating: 1-5 (5 being the highest)   0   1   2   3   4   5

Plan:

<u>Showing Compassion</u>
Colossians 3:12 *Put on therefore, as the elect of God, holy and beloved, bowels of mercies, kindness, humbleness of mind, meekness, longsuffering;*

Goal:

Current Rating: 1-5 (5 being the highest)   0   1   2   3   4   5

Plan:

<u>V. Transformation (Romans 8:28)</u>

Romans 12:2 *And be not **conformed** to this world: but be ye **transformed** by the renewing of your mind, that ye may prove what is that good, and acceptable, and perfect, will of God.*

<u>Filled and lead by the Spirit</u>

Ephesians 5:18 *And be not drunk with wine, wherein is excess; but **be filled with the Spirit**;*

Goal:

Current Rating: 1-5 (5 being the highest)   0   1   2   3   4   5

Plan:

Showing love: Edifying, encouraging thoughts & Words- self and others
Ephesians 4:29 Let no corrupt communication proceed out of your mouth, but that which is good to the use of **edifying**, that it may **minister grace** unto the hearers.

Goal

Current Rating: 1-5 (5 being the highest)   0   1   2   3   4   5

Plan:

Engage in opportunities to nurture someone's spiritual growth
Matthew 28:19 Go ye therefore, **and teach** all nations, baptizing them in the name of the Father, and of the Son, and of the Holy Ghost:

Goal:

Current Rating: 1-5 (5 being the highest)   0   1   2   3   4   5

Plan:

Turning negatives into positives
2 Corinthians 10:4- 5 (For the weapons of our warfare are not carnal, but mighty through God to the pulling down of strong holds;) Casting down imaginations, and every high thing that exalteth itself against the knowledge of God, and bringing into captivity every thought to the obedience of Christ;

Goal:

Current Rating: 1-5 (5 being the highest)   0   1   2   3   4   5

Plan:

INTRODUCTION

Nowadays there is a plan for everything! For everything that we deem important, someone has developed an "approved" and "certifiable" plan. There is financial planning, physical wellness planning, marriage planning, birth planning, funeral planning, maintenance planning and menu planning. All these plans and many more are found in abundance. Yet for the most important area of all...where's the plan? Is spiritual growth not important enough to have a plan? Jesus and His Apostles seem to think it is (Luke 14:25-34, 2 Corinthians 3:18 & 2 Peter 1:8)!

Spiritual Growth is indeed important! Do you have a plan? In this book, a trusted pastor and former chaplain details and explains the twenty categories of spiritual growth that every believer should recognize, and every pastor or disciple maker should be measuring. Over and over again God's Word admonishes us to grow! This admonition is explicitly in scriptures like **1 Peter 2:2** *"As newborn babes, desire the sincere milk of the word, that ye may grow thereby:"* and **2 Peter 3:18** *"But grow in grace, and in the knowledge of our Lord and Saviour Jesus Christ. To him be glory both now and for ever. Amen"*. And it is implicit in scriptures like **Luke 8:8** *"And other fell on good ground, and sprang up, and bare fruit an hundredfold. And when he had said these things, he cried, He that hath ears to hear, let him hear"* and **Colossians 1:10** *"That ye might walk worthy of the Lord unto all pleasing, being fruitful in every good work, and increasing in the knowledge of God;"*. Spiritual growth is more than numeric growth and cannot be regulated to a single Bible study. It is progressive, multifaceted, interpersonal and ongoing. Each of the five levels under which the twenty categories are arranged are progressive in nature. In other words, you should seek to master the first before moving on to the next. For example, if you have a hard time denying yourself then carrying a cross will be impossible!

The Spiritual Growth Plan is a tool, intended to help you grow up spiritually. Ultimately, under the expert guidance of the Holy Spirit it will assist in conforming you to the image of Christ (Romans 8:29). It is not legalistic, nor is it intended to condemn, but rather to encourage and provide measurable feedback to the believer who wants to grow spiritually. It is not intended in any way to replace Christian discipleship but rather supplement and guide the discipleship process. Like any tool, it's only good if you use it; but it is guaranteed that if you prayerfully and faithfully work the Spiritual Growth Plan as it is shared here it will work for you and YOU WILL GROW!

SPIRITUAL GROWTH PLAN
Discussion Questions:

Who says you need to plan for your spiritual growth?

What are the areas of concern regarding spiritual growth?

When do you know you are growing spiritually?

Where are the areas that need the most attention in your life?

Why is it important to plan for your spiritual growth?

How do you plan to grow spiritually (Be as specific as possible)?

1. SELF-DENIAL

AFTER THE NEW BIRTH, self-denial is the first step of the spiritual growth process. And of course, it is, because it was self that got us in our mess in the first place. Genesis 3:6 says, "And when the woman saw that the tree was *good for food*, and that it was *pleasant to the eyes*, and a tree to be *desired to make one wise*, she took of the fruit thereof, and did eat, and gave also unto her husband with her; and he did eat (italics added)." It was the selfish will of Adam and Eve that got us in this cursed predicament to begin with. This is something we received straight from Satan who stirred the selfish nature of mankind (Gen. 3:4-5) just as his own selfish conceit had prompted his own rebellion (Isaiah 14:13-14). Our selfish response to his proposition allowed sin to defile the world (Romans 5:12). And our desires for the things of this world have been defiled ever since. 1 John 2:16 confirms this when it says, "For all that is in the world, the *lust of the flesh*, and the *lust of the eyes*, and the *pride of life*, is *not of the Father*, but is of the world (italics added)." Our selfishness is so bad that it heads the list of perils of the last days. 2 Timothy 3:1-2 say, *"This know also, that in the last days perilous times shall come.2 For men shall be* **lovers of their own selves***, covetous, boasters, proud, blasphemers, disobedient to parents, unthankful, unholy..."*

The very first requirement that Jesus placed on His disciples was that they deny themselves by leaving their old lives behind, forsaking what they were accustomed to all their lives. This is recorded in each of the synoptic Gospels (Matthew 4:20-22; Mark 1:18- 20 & Luke 5:27-28). Mark 8:34 records the demands of Jesus, "And when he had called the people unto him with his disciples also, he said unto them, Whosoever will come after me, let him deny himself, and take up his cross, and follow me"(see also Matthew 16:24 and Luke 9:23). Then in the same breath He says, "For whosoever will save his life shall lose it: and whosoever will lose his life for my sake shall find it" (Matthew

16:25-see also Mark 8:35 and Luke 9:24). We can safely deduce from these scriptures that to be a follower of Jesus... you must deny yourself!

When you research the word "self", you will find that this same "self" is often substituted in the Bible with the word "flesh", not the flesh of our bodies but the inner will of man that is contrary to the will of God. Galatians 5:17 says, "For the flesh lusteth against the Spirit, and the Spirit against the flesh: and these are contrary the one to the other: so that ye cannot do the things that ye would". The Bible declares that it is this very same flesh that makes God angry and makes us deserve of His judgement. Ephesians 2:3 says, "Among whom also we all had our conversation in times past in the lusts of our flesh, fulfilling the desires of the flesh and of the mind; and were by nature the children of wrath, even as others". It is the flesh that makes us God's enemies (Romans 8:7 and James 4:4)!

We should not trust the flesh (Jeremiah 17:5). We should not love the flesh (Jude 1:23). We should hate the flesh (Ezekiel 36:31). We should not only deny it but we should run from it for dear life and crucify it with its passions (Galatians 5:24) every chance we get! What are you doing with your flesh? What are you doing with your selfish desires? Are you fighting the good fight of faith or are you putting up a fight at all? The wisest thing you can do is to acknowledge that you will give an account for everything you do and begin to do what God wants you to do. Deny yourself and put God first and in the end, you'll be glad that you did.

SELF DENIAL
Discussion Questions:

Who does Jesus say we must deny and why (Matthew 16:23-25 & Luke 9:23)?

What does it mean to deny "self" (Galatians 6:7-11)?

When are you most tempted to allow the self to take center stage (Luke 4:13)?

From where do evil desires come (Jeremiah 17:9 & James 4:1)?

Why is self /flesh such a persistent foe (Judges 2:22-23, Romans 7:15-17 & Galatians 5:17)?

How can one get consistent victory over the flesh (Rom 8:13, Col 3:5 & Gal 5:24)?

ACKNOWLEDGING GOD

SINNERS (THOSE OUTSIDE OF fellowship with God) seek *their* wants and needs and include God only as a means of accomplishing *their* goals. Believers; however, are seekers of God, longing to please Him and accomplish His goals above their own. This is apparent in Matthew 6:32 as Jesus describes how the perspective, principles and priorities of the hypocrites and heathens are all wrong. They act as if there was not a Heavenly Father that already knew their needs and was willing to be their supply. Jesus then proceeds to instruct His followers to have a different perspective, operate on different principles and have different priorities with Christ having preeminence as their King. Disciples of Christ are citizens of His Kingdom and while forsaking this world, they are to "seek ye first the kingdom of God, and his righteousness; and all these things shall be added unto you" (Matthew 6:33). You cannot seek the kingdom without consulting with the King!

You may ask, how do I consult with the King? No appointment is necessary, you can call Him up at any time and He's happy to make house calls. Prayer is the answer. Prayer in its purest form is simply communication with God. But true communication requires two or more parties to commune, that is to share intimate thoughts and feelings. True communication also requires the sharing of both parties in both directions. You cannot do all the talking, never listen, read (God's Word) or look for non-spoken language (circumstances, signs and special sayings) and consider it communication. All you've done was have a conversation with yourself (Luke 18:11).

Instead of you doing all the talking during prayer, you should take time to listen for the voice of the Lord. You should also search the Scriptures to see if the King has already addressed the issue you're dealing with in prayer. If you are not that familiar with the Bible, seek godly counsel from Christians with good reputations for giving good advice and living godly lives. Oftentimes these people are already in authority over your local church. Sometimes these

Christian are no longer in the flesh, so we have to read books on their thoughts and experiences (this is like the King's case law). Finally, when you decide that you must have an answer regardless of the cost, it's time to fast. Fasting is a way to supercharge your prayer life. It overtly announces that you are prioritizing your prayer concern above the things of the world.

In summary, to acknowledge God we must go to Him as our Creator and King and ask what He thinks about the decisions we make. In addition to asking we must 1) search the scriptures for what is already "on the books" 2) seek answers in quiet reflection, 3) pay attention to circumstances, signs and the special things that are said (often repeated), 4) seek godly counsel in other Christians and their related experiences (King's case law) and finally through the 5) spiritual discipline known as fasting. If this is done with passion and attention to what the Bible says is proper (James 5:16 & John 14:13-14), you will not only acknowledge God but He will acknowledge you and grant you your petition (1 John 5:14-15).

ACKNOWLEDGING GOD
Discussion Questions

Who is the most important person in your life (hint: who you think of, talk to and spend time with the most IS the most important person in your life whether you admit it or not)?

What does it mean to acknowledge God?

When do you know you have adequately acknowledged God?

Where in scripture do you see examples of acknowledging God?

Why is acknowledging God primary?

How do you plan to acknowledge God in more areas or a greater degree in your life?

REPENTANCE

REPENT. THE WORD APPEARS in some form or another over one hundred times in the Bible. It appears to be a prerequisite for salvation. By definition it is remorse or contrition over one's past action. But feeling bad doesn't quite capture the full meaning of repentance. The Bible describes both a godly sorrow that convicts and brings to life as opposed to a worldly sorrow which condemns and makes you kill yourself. Examples of godly sorrow or real repentance include Jacob, David and Peter. Examples of worldly sorrow include Esau, Pharaoh and Judas. It is a change of mind, but it is much more than that. Repentance is nothing short of a complete change in your being that proves out in your behavior. Biblical repentance and Biblical faith are two sides of the same coin. Just as faith without works is dead so repentance without change (turning from dead works and turning toward life) is incomplete.

John the Baptist preached it. Jesus preached it. He sent out the twelve preaching it. He sent out the seventy other disciples preaching it. Paul calls it a foundational or fundamental principle of Christ. Repentance is not only fundamental, but it is the gift and will of God! We must repent not only of the things we do that are in opposition to God's will for our lives, but we must repent from not doing the things we know we should. James 4:17 says, "Therefore to him that knoweth to do good, and doeth it not, to him it is sin". Also, a thought to consider is that delayed obedience is disobedience. Repent is a present tense word. Time spent not doing what is right is time spent doing what is wrong.

Repentance typically follows confrontation and conviction, which is a revelation that you're in the wrong and a resolve not to be found there again. Yet you do not have to wait for a feeling from God to repent. Anytime you are confronted with truth that exposes an incongruence between how you believe and behave versus God's Will as revealed in His Word you have the right and responsibility to repent. No one ever said that repenting is easy. The truth, especially about ourselves, often hurts. But thank God it also heals! And in order to be right with God and not suffer the consequences of our own ways, repentance is necessary.

It seems in our modern era that true repentance has gone out of style. It's often the punchlines in jokes and situational comedy that someone "finds religion" and changes their ways. Yet regardless of public perception, repentance is healthy. It can be said to serve in the soul as the plumbing serves in a house. Through repentance all the unclean stuff gets washed and flushed away. Jesus said He's coming back for a church (called out individuals) without spot or wrinkle. You may ask, how much should you repent? I would ask, how clean do you want to be? And why stay dirty when Christ shed His blood to make you clean?

Repentance not only cleanses, but it changes. Repentance not only changes but considers. It considers the consequences one's actions have on others and on God. True repentance will make it nearly impossible to return to your previous condition. All of this is challenging but if you avail yourself in faith to the challenge God has promised that you'll wear a crown. Seven times in the book of Revelation God promises reward for those who overcome. But you can't overcome staying in the same situation and you can't overcome until you come over and agree with what God says about your experience. Agree with God… repent… and receive the reward He's been ever so eager to endow upon you!

REPENTANCE
Discussion Questions

Who needs to repent?

What is repentance?

When do you know that repentance is genuine and complete?

Where does the Bible say we must repent from the things we are neglecting to do?

Why is repentance vital to spiritual growth?

How do you intend to incorporate repentance as part and parcel of your life?

OVERCOMING TEMPTATION

TEMPTATION IS A NORMAL part of the Christian life. Being tempted is not a sin (Matthew 4:1, Mark 1:13, Luke 4:2 & Hebrews 2:18; 4:15) but what you do when you are tempted is what you will have to give an account for before God (Romans 14:12 & 2 Corinthians 5:10). In order to grow spiritually you must see every temptation and every sin for what it really is. Temptation is simply an opportunity. Sin is a betrayal of love, trust and allegiance. The Devil wants to use the opportunity to get you to sin, thereby trapping you (Mark 6:21; 14:11, Luke 4:13). God; however, uses the opportunity to test you. The Devil's trap (no matter how enticing, reasonable, or familiar) is designed to destroy you, whereas the Lord's test is purposed to promote you. When you are tempted you are given the opportunity to succumb to Satan's seduction and rebel against God or to prove yourself worthy of God's promotion. Overcoming temptation is a prerequisite for power. It's the choices you make before and during temptation that determine whether the opportunity is a blessing or a curse (Deuteronomy 11:26 & 30:19).

We all know that "the devil is busy"! But one thing you must know is that the devil has boundaries. Unlike God, the devil, nor his demons can be everywhere all the time (there are less demons than angels anyway, 1/3 versus 2/3 (Revelation 12:4 & 2 Kings 6:16). So, they don't have time to bother anybody that doesn't pose a threat to their kingdom, their agenda or their power. They will, however, possess, oppress, depress, suppress and impress whoever pops up on the Kingdom of Darkness' list of enemies to the state. The more you manifest that the victory is won, the more you become public enemy number one. Whether you know it or not, Satan can see what God is sending your way and He deploys resources specifically to keep your blessing away (**Daniel 10:13**)!

The more of a threat you are the more resources are allocated to deal with you (Satan himself showed up to challenge Jesus)! That is where temptation enters the scene. **Temptation** is simply any attempt by enemy forces to block, rock, or stop what God is doing in your life.

The very first thing many people experience when they think of temptation is fear! This is due to cultural conditioning that has "chumped" you into being a coward rather than the conqueror God made you to be. Most people begin to think of the gross, obscene, gigantic moral failures that cause calamity in life. But temptation usually comes in a much more subtle and crafty way (Genesis 3:1). Temptation comes to merely get you a little off track from where God wants to take you. The further God wants to take you, the more difference a little deviation makes. Whenever presented with a thought, choice or opportunity you have the option to accept or reject depending on your dominant desire. You only discipline yourself when your desire for what you want is greater than your desire for what you currently have. That's why God gave you His spirit! He's blessed you with different desires so you can be, have and do better! 2 Timothy 1:7 in the Amplified Bible (AMP) says, "For God did not give us a spirit of timidity or cowardice or fear, but [He has given us a spirit] of power and of love and of sound judgment and personal discipline [abilities that result in a calm, well-balanced mind and self-control]". In Matthew 4:1-11 we have the greatest example of overcoming temptation ever recorded. Jesus, our ultimate example in all things pleasing to God, overcame temptation through vision, decision and discipline. That's how He walked into His destiny, giving us the greatest example of how to overcome temptation and stay on track for the destination God has for us.

Before we can live a life that is pleasing to God, we must know what a life that pleases God looks like. That's where **vision** takes center stage. Vision is seeing beyond where you are to where God is taking you. **Proverbs 29:18** (NIV)18 Where there is no revelation (***vision***), people cast off restraint (exercise no discipline); but blessed is the one who heeds (***submit to, commits to, discipline oneself in accordance with***) wisdom's instruction. God's vision for you is synonymous with your identity in Him! That's why in Matthew chapter 3 God declared who Jesus was before he sent Him into the wilderness to be challenged. The revelation Jesus had of Himself gave Him the motivation to discipline Himself and refuse what the enemy offered.

If you want your plans to succeed you must ensure that your plans align with God's plans. **Proverbs 19:21** (NIV) says, "Many are the plans in a person's heart, but it is the Lord's purpose that prevails." God will not support you if what you do does not support Him. Your vision cannot be just to be happy or feel good. You could be happy or feel good with something bad for you! You could be happy and feel good with something killing your vision. You could be happy and feel good with something in direct opposition to God's will for your life! Pleasure without purpose will cause you to perish! Vision keeps you on track. Vision makes you not want to turn back. Vision makes the real choices plain to see. Vision makes decisions easy!

Whenever God gives you a vision, Satan comes to divide that vision, causing division. This division is the mission of temptation. Matthew 13:19 says, "When any one heareth the word of the kingdom, and understandeth it not, then cometh the wicked one, and catcheth away that which was sown in his heart. This is he which received seed by the wayside." John 10:10 says, "The thief cometh not, but for to steal, and to kill, and to destroy: I am come that they might have life, and that they might have it more abundantly." God has a vision for you and whenever your vision is to be delivered, the devil has a vision of your destruction. God has a vision of you being a conqueror, the devil has a vision of you remaining conquered. God has a vision of your success; the devil has a vision to keep you subdued. You have to make the decision, with whom to align your vision.

Your vision will be determined, more than anything else by your decisions! You can cancel any plot of the devil with one decision and with one decision you can change the course of your destiny. The power to decide is the greatest power there is! Decision is the power to choose the direction of your life. God has all the power to accomplish all things but if you don't decide that you want what He wants then you'll never get what He has for you. Decision is more than making a choice. If you simply make a choice you will change as soon as it is challenged. But if you make a decision the way Jesus makes decisions then your choice is more than a choice- it is a commitment! When you make a commitment, you stay the course and do not change. That is what it takes to run this Christian race and win. This commitment to a vision is what we call discipline.

Discipline is self-imposed activities and restrictions one commits themselves to in order to accomplish a vision. Discipline is a decision to live now, not for now, but to live now for later! **Hebrews 11:25** says, "Choosing rather to suffer affliction with the people of God, than to enjoy the pleasures of sin for a season;" **Hebrews 12:11** says, "Now no chastening for the present seemeth to be joyous, but grievous: nevertheless afterward it yieldeth the peaceable fruit of righteousness unto them which are exercised thereby. Discipline is temptation's antidote.

OVERCOMING TEMPTATION
Discussion Questions

Who suffers when you give into temptation?

What is the goal of temptation (John 10:10)?

When are you most vulnerable to temptation (James 1:14)?

Where do you go to escape temptation (Psalm 61:2 & 1 Corinthians 10:13)?

Why do you think you are tempted with the particular things with which you are?

How do you plan to overcome the thing that's been over you?

PRAISE IN THE MIDST OF PROBLEMS

PRAISE IS A PECULIAR thing! Praise is a physical expression that has spiritual power! Praise is both a noun and a verb. Praise is a communication (*n*) of admiration, approval, respect, reverence and gratitude. But to be complete praise must be expressed (*v*). This expression is always visible. It is never silent… it is never still. Praise is on display for all of creation to see! Praise is an act of war and defiance against your enemy.

Everybody should praise God (Psalm 150:6) but God's peculiar people (Exodus 19:5, Deuteronomy 14:2, Psalm 135:4, Titus 2:14) are especially purposed to praise Him (Psalm 33:1, Ephesians 1:2-12 & 1 Peter 2:9) because our praise glorifies God.

Praise not only glorifies God, but praise is the vehicle that takes you to God (Psalm 100:4) and gets the enemy off your back! No matter how the devil has you down, praise will confuse your enemy (2 Chronicles 20:22), set you free (Acts 16:25) and lift you up (Psalm 24)!

In Hebrew there were at least seven different words for praise (**Halal** (celebrate. from which we get Hallelujah), **Yadah** (extend hands), **Towdah** (extend hands), **Shabach** (shout), **Barak** (kneel down), **Zamar** (play instruments) and **Tehillah** (sing)) to express in several ways our faith in God! We must use every weapon in our arsenal to overcome the world, the flesh and the devil. Praise is easy when things go well but to grow spiritually, you must learn to praise in the midst of problems.

Praise God in the midst of problems? You might say, "That doesn't make sense"! Well, the Gospel doesn't make sense to those perishing but to the saved it is the power of God (1 Corinthians 1:18)! It doesn't make sense for God to leave His throne in Heaven to die on a rugged cross for man (Philippians 2:7), BUT HE DID IT! It doesn't make sense for one to die for the sins of many (Romans 5:15-19), BUT HE DID IT! It doesn't make sense for Him who had no sin to become sin for us (2 Corinthians 5:21) BUT HE DID IT! Now can you see how you can praise Him despite your problems!? For all He has done, is doing and will do for you…what are you willing to do for Him, will you praise Him!

You may say, I want to praise but my problems prohibit me (weigh me down). Know this, that problems will persist for those who do not press into praise. Praise is often a sacrifice (Psalm 49:14-16 and Hebrews 13:15). Most importantly, praise is an act of volition. You must choose to praise God. No one can make you praise God, but you must always choose to praise God. It is a spiritual act where the spirit impresses upon the will and you make the conscious decision to praise your God! It is an act of faith toward God that says despite my problems, God, you're worthy of praise!

In Psalm 103:1 David wrote, "Bless the Lord, O my soul: and all that is within me, bless his holy name". When David commanded His soul to bless the Lord, he understood that He was a triune being, spirit, soul and body. The body will naturally follow the dictates of the soul (mind, will and emotions) but the soul will only obey the dictates of God when the spirit is in charge! Like David, from your spirit you can command your soul and the body will follow! This is a choice that can be made at any time, in any situation! You don't have to wait until you're in church, or for your body to feel good or for things to go your way. You can bless the Lord at all times. In good times, in bad times, in in-between times…bless the Lord (Psalm 34:1)!

Praise says that you have a higher perspective than just what you're going through! Praise says you know that one way or another God is going to see you through! And if for no other reason, you praise God because He is worthy, (2 Samuel 22:4) because He is great (1 Chronicles 16:25), and because He is good (2 Chronicles 5:13)!

There was a time when the saints would stand up during testimony service and boldly declare; that they wanted to thank God for waking them up in their right mind and starting them on their way! They thanked God for giving them the facilities of their limbs, one more chance and yet another day. They reminded their audience that He didn't have to do it but HE DID IT anyway. And they were careful to make known that it wasn't because of any goodness of their own but because He was just good…all the time…and all the time… GOD IS GOOD!

If after all that, you find your mind is bankrupt of praise and you are struggling to find anything for which to give thanks. It's time to borrow praise from a song, a sermon, a poem or a psalm (the Bible's book of praise). Praise Him on credit! Praise Him in advance! Praise Him because He has a track record of bringing His Word to pass! Prepare your mind and purpose in your heart to do what you were created to do. To press through the storm, to endure the pain, to see past the fog, and do whatever it takes to praise your God in Jesus' Name!

PRAISE IN THE MIDST OF PROBLEMS:
Discussion Questions

Who should praise God?

What does praise do?

When should one praise God?

Where does praise penetrate?

Why does pride prohibit praise?

How can you make your praise perpetual?

11. CROSS BEARING

NOT LONG AGO IN Charleston, SC I was driving over Interstate 26 when I noticed a man literally carrying a cross! He had not been beaten or made to do so; it was not a sign of punishment nor was it too heavy. As a matter of fact, it was on wheels and had a sign attached to it that said, "Jesus saves". I thought to myself, "Now that guy is *serious* about carrying his cross for Jesus!" No matter how you choose to do it, bearing a cross is part and parcel of following Jesus Christ! If you want to grow in God and get to all God has for you, you must go the way of the cross (Matthew 10:38). The cross was essential to Jesus' message (Mark 8:34) and it was essential to the message of the early Church (1 Peter 2:24). The cross was so essential that Paul said to the Corinthians that He would focus on nothing else (1 Corinthians 2:2).

Cross bearing is more than wearing a necklace or bracelet with a miniaturized cross dangling from it. And despite the Charleston man's dedication, it's more than pulling a cross down the street on your back. Where self-denial is, for the sake of Christ, not allowing yourself the privilege that you are otherwise entitled to; cross bearing is, for the sake of Christ, taking on responsibility that you otherwise would not do. Cross bearing is when you do, not because someone is making you, not because you have to, not even because you want to, but you do **to please and serve** the One who died for you!

In Jesus' day the cross was literally made of wood and nails but today your cross may be figurative. Your "cross" involves any sacrificial aspect of life that you choose to carry in the spirit and for the glory of God. Cross bearing involves acts of service, being obedient, persevering through adversity and making peace.

God often calls people to do things they didn't want to do. The Bible is replete with examples such as; Abraham, Moses, Joseph, Children of Israel, Barack, Jeremiah, Isaiah, Ezekiel, Esther, Peter, Onesimus and on and on! Cross bearing is simply God's road to spiritual growth. As William Penn put it, "No pain, no palm; no thorns, no throne; no gall, no glory; no cross, no crown." Now, before you throw in the towel, just because God's best requires something of you, consider the alternative and know that whatever you do, God will be the one to reward you (Ephesians 6:8). Also, you will have to give an account for all you do (Romans 14:12) and only what you do for Christ will last (1 Corinthians 15:58).

But know this, your labor is not in vain! Seven times to the seven churches of the book of Revelation, God said, "I know your works". Like Boaz noticed Ruth (Ruth 2:11), God notices when you are doing things for His sake, especially when you don't have to do it. Jesus didn't have to do it but He looked to His reward (Hebrews 12:2). As we follow Jesus down the same road of the cross He traveled, the Bible promises that we too will receive our just reward (2 Timothy 2:12 & 4:8). Isn't it only right that we should follow the Captain of our souls? Like the words of the famous hymnal, "Must Jesus bear the cross alone, and all the world go free? No, there's a cross for everyone, And there's a cross for me."

Confession: *Galatians 2:20 I am crucified with Christ: nevertheless I live; yet not I, but Christ liveth in me: and the life which I now live in the flesh I live by the faith of the Son of God, who loved me, and gave himself for me.*

CROSS BEARING:
Discussion Questions

Who is called to bear a cross?

What is cross bearing?

When are you expected to pick up your cross?

Where do you see opportunities for cross bearing?

Why is cross bearing profitable?

How do you intend to instigate God glorifying cross bearing?

SERVICE

GOD REALLY DOES LOVE you! He loved you so much that He sent Jesus to die for you. But God didn't save you from Hell just to give you a ticket to Heaven. If the only reason for Christ to die was to have you with Him in Heaven, you would have died the moment you were saved! God left you here on earth for a period of time to use you to His glory. The sooner you realize your purpose on earth, the sooner you can get on with what God has for you. Not only were you saved for love, but you were <u>Saved 2 Serve</u>!

God is serious about your service! God is so serious about your service that He gave the Holy Spirit to equip you to serve. This equipping comes in the form of Spiritual gifts. Spiritual gifts can be seen as artillery against the kingdom of darkness. Like a soldier is equipped for a physical war, God has equipped us for the spiritual war that we face. Like a builder to whom the right tool is essential in getting the job done right. God expects us to use our spiritual gifts in ever increasing ways to get the job that He has assigned to us done right! Like a farmer equipped with the specific seed to produce the desired harvest, God does not want you to be without what you need to accomplish His will for your life. That's why He gives seed to the sower and that's why He gives gifts to you so through spiritual gifts you are <u>Equipped 2 Serve</u>!

Notice that of all the spiritual gifts, all but one is designed to minister grace to someone else (1 Corinthians 12, Romans 12, Ephesians 4 & 1 Peter 4). That's because your gift is not for you but rather to bless someone else. In the plan of God your participation is required because God works through people to bless people. Jesus, the Captain of our souls (Hebrews 2:10), after having washed the disciple's feet, said, "Now that I, your Lord and Teacher, have washed your feet, you also should wash one another's feet. I have set you an example that you should do as I have done for you." Feet washing was the humblest of service and Jesus was telling us that we are <u>Required 2 serve</u>.

Vision for your life is attached to your service. Ephesians 2:10 NIV says, "For we are God's handiwork, created in Christ Jesus to do good works, which God prepared in advance for us to do". The Bible says, "Where there is no vision, the people perish…". Where there is no revelation, people cast off restraint (Proverbs 29:18). That means that without vision people tend to get involved with all kinds of activities that don't do them any good, leaving them in a mess of meaninglessness. This is the opposite of discipline which directs the individual to destiny's doorstep. To get to where God has gifted you, you must have God's <u>Vision 2 serve</u>.

Engagement is required to serve. Mark 2:5 says, "When Jesus saw their faith, he said unto the sick of the palsy, Son, thy sins be forgiven thee" Faith that is not seen is not faith at all. . James 2:18 says "Yea, a man may say, Thou hast faith, and I have works: shew me thy faith without thy works, and I will shew thee my faith by my works." If you suspect that you're of service but no one sees your service, then you're probably of no service at all. This is scary for many because it's so much easier to be served or to criticize the service of others rather than get out front and actually serve. But when you don't you deprive others of your contribution and defraud yourself of God's opportunities. Matthew 14:29 says, "And he said, Come. And when Peter was come down out of the ship, he walked on the water, to go to Jesus. You never know what you can do until you step out of your comfort zone and see what God wants to do through you…you must be <u>Engaged 2 serve</u>.

SERVICE:
Discussion Questions

Who does Jesus say are the greatest in the kingdom of God?

What is your spiritual gift?

When do you share what God has put in you?

Where do you see greater opportunities for service?

Why is service so important?

How do you intend to be a more successful servant?

OBEDICENCE

OPEN HEAVEN. THAT'S RIGHT! An open heaven is promised to all those who obey the commands of God (Deuteronomy 28:12). An open Heaven is indicative of such a right relationship with God where God is free to bless, and you are free to receive. An open heaven is the mode through which God's best for your life is channeled (Malachi 3:10). Revelation 4:1 says, "After this I looked, and, behold, *a door* was **opened** in **heaven**:" That's right! When you are living in obedience to God's revealed will for your life, He will literally open a door in heaven (Revelation 3:8) and do for you and show to you (Ezekiel 1:1) things hidden from everyone else but revealed to you because of your obedience (Genesis 22:18).

Now just as sure as there's a Heaven, there's a Hell. There's an open heaven that is accessed through obedience, and there is a closed heaven (hell) that is the result of sin and disobedience (Deuteronomy 11:17). But God in His gracious mercy allows for U-turns in life, we call this repentance (1 Kings 8:35-36). Yet even in repenting, the call is to obey.

Obedience is so very important to the life of the believer. Obedience is more than a mere act. It is an attitude. It is belief that becomes behavior that results in blessing. You will never get any further in God than your last act of obedience (Exodus 4:26 & Joshua 5). Regardless of how we may want to barter and bargain with God, blessing, true blessing from God, is designed to follow obedience not precede it (Isaiah 1:19).

Not only will you not go any further in God than your last act of obedience, because sin separates us from the Blesser we cannot enjoy God while we are yet in disobedience (Proverbs 13:15). When we are in sin, we have a hard time entering into the presence of the Lord. So, we miss out on all that is in His presence. Psalm 16:11 says, "Thou wilt shew me the path of life: in thy presence is fullness of joy; at thy right hand there are pleasures for evermore."

Disobedience and sin stunt your spiritual life but obedience is always followed by blessing. It pays to obey!

OBEDIENCE:
Discussion Questions

Who benefits most from your obedience?

What does obedience open that is otherwise closed?

When do blessings overtake you? Deuteronomy 28:2 & Psalm 23

Where does obedience begin? Matthew 15:19

Why is it important to discipline your mind? 2 Corinthians 10:5

How can you overcome disobedience in your life?

PERSEVERANCE

EVERY WORTHWHILE ENDEAVOR REQUIRES perseverance to complete. From invention to repair and from birth to maturity- purposeful, planned, persistent effort makes the difference between success and failure. Spiritual growth is no exception! We are encouraged again and again in God's Word to persevere. Peter, Paul, John and Jesus all admonish us to persevere. The Bible uses words like "endure, patience, suffer, continue, longsuffering, vigilance and diligence" to articulate the concept of perseverance. Some versions of the Bible call diligence, a synonym of persistence, mankind's precious possession (Proverbs 12:27 AMP, NKJV). According to the Merriam Webster dictionary, perseverance is defined as continued effort to do or achieve something despite difficulties, failure, or opposition. Four words stand out in that definition: continued, effort, achieve & despite.

Continued...Some things don't happen right away but must be continued for a period of time before any substantial success is realized. Education, farming, athletic ability and many other things work that way and so does spiritual growth. James 1:25 says, "But whoso looketh into the perfect law of liberty, and **continueth** therein, he being not a forgetful hearer, but a doer of the work, this man shall be blessed in his deed". Faith is not enough (2 Peter 1:5)! Without persistence your faith will fail (Luke 22:32 & Colossians 1:23). Giving God time is key to inheriting His promises (Hebrews 6:12). Too often, too many saints give up too easily! Just imagine what life would have been like had you not given up on the desire God put in your heart (Matthew 23:37 & Luke 13:34)!

Effort...Many Christians mistakenly believe that if an endeavor is of God it will be easy and automatic. This is sometimes true but more often than not this is not the case. God requires our participation for His purpose to prevail in our lives (Exodus 3:7, Matthew 28:19-20 & Mark 16:20). That participation must by necessity be our best effort (Mark 12:30-31, Luke 10:27). Half-baked, half-hearted attempts just won't do (2 Kings 13:19 & Revelation 3:16)! God has established the spiritual principle of sowing and reaping (Genesis 8:22 & Galatians 6:7-9). Be sure to do your part when it comes to the plans of God for your life. Your efforts for God will not go unnoticed (Revelation 2:2) nor will they go unrewarded (Matthew 16:27 & Mark 9:41).

Achieve…Many Christians feel like achievement is somehow inconsistent with humility and God's grace, but nothing could be further from the truth (Matthew 25:21-23 & 2 Cor 5:10; 20)! Hebrews 6:15 says, "And so, after he had patiently endured, he obtained the promise". Anyone can achieve anything by God's grace, given enough time and effort (Matt 19:26, Luke 18:27 & Philippians 4:13)! God wants you to achieve and is standing ready with your reward after you do (Matthew 16:26-27, Romans 2:7 & 1 Peter 5:10).

Despite…Someone who understands despite doesn't ignore or imagine that challenges don't exist. Someone who has an attitude of despite just decides to press past the pain of the cross so that they can enjoy the celebration of the crown (2 Corinthians 2:12). I like to call it having a "nevertheless" in your spirit. In Matthew 26:39 the Bible says, (also recorded in Mark 14:36 & Luke 22:42) "And he went a little farther, and fell on his face, and prayed, saying, O my Father, if it be possible, let this cup pass from me: **nevertheless** not as I will, but as thou wilt." Jesus, the Son of God had to suffer and in the midst of it He chose to say, "NEVERTHELESS". That is the tipping point, that is where the rubber meets the road, that is having the Spirit of Christ. Having a "nevertheless" in your spirit! When you have a "nevertheless" in your spirit nothing the Devil throws at you can stop you because you've conquered everything He could find on the inside to persuade, discourage or move you (Psalm 62:2, John 14:30 & 1 Corinthians 15:58)! When you have a nevertheless in your spirit, you remind yourself that God is working all things together for your good (Romans 8:28)! When you have a nevertheless in your spirit, you remember that He is faithful and will not allow you to be tempted more than you can bear (1 Corinthians 10:13). You remember that "trouble doesn't last always". That though weeping may endure for a night, joy comes in the morning (Psalm 30:5)! And no matter how bad it gets GOD IS STILL GOOD!

God looks for opportunities to show Himself strong on our behalf, but His show of strength is most evident when the odds are against us (2 Chronicles 16:9, 2 Cor 12:9). In order to fully see and realize God's purpose for our lives we must be looking as well. Hebrews 12:2 says, "Looking unto Jesus the author and finisher of our faith; who for the joy that was set before him endured the cross, despising the shame, and is set down at the right hand of the throne of God". We must look and continue to look to Jesus until our joy is fulfilled. That is the secret to persistence and persistence is the secret to your success.

PERSISTENCE:
Discussion Questions

Who is responsible for your response?

What areas in your life require persistence?

When is persistence necessary?

Where do you look in order to overcome?

Why does God make persistence a prerequisite for success?

How do you intend to exercise your effort to accomplish God's goals?

PEACEMAKING

PERHAPS THE FIRST RULE of spiritual growth is that the kingdom of God doesn't work like the kingdom of darkness (the world). In a world that the Bible calls "untoward" (Acts 2:40), peacemaking isn't popular. Many people actually pride themselves on being self-proclaimed "hellraisers". You know the type, who won't forgive, who think arguing is a thrill, and who will hold a grudge as long as they live (Leviticus 19:18). Nevertheless, if you want to grow spiritually, you have to find a better way! Paul said, "yet shew I unto you a more excellent way." (1 Corinthians 12:31). Jesus said, "you have heard it said but I say to you" (Matthew 5:38-48). And Isaiah said "For my thoughts are not your thoughts, neither are your ways my ways, saith the Lord. For as the heavens are higher than the earth, so are my ways higher than your ways, and my thoughts than your thoughts" (Isaiah 55:8-9). So, if you want to operate like God you cannot operate like the world! Thank God there's a better way!

In every situation we have an option to choose which alternative of reality to bring to pass in our lives (Joshua 24:15). In this ability to choose we have been given the power to affect future outcomes (Deuteronomy 30:19). When we recognize this power, we have the responsibility to choose wisely... to choose peace (Galatians 6:7). The Devil does not want you to choose peace. He wants you to operate on the principles of the world so he can continue to take advantage of your fleshly ignorance (2 Corinthians 2:11). He specializes in confusion, division, disorder, darkness, discord and wrath (Galatians 5:19-21). Unfortunately, this is normal to many people. Hence, divide and conquer is the strategy the Devil utilizes (Zechariah 3 & Revelation 12:10). He wants you to see people as adversaries instead of partners. But we must always remember, "we wrestle not against flesh and blood, but against principalities, against powers, against the rulers of the darkness of this world, against spiritual wickedness in high places" (Ephesians 6:12). We often don't see peace as an option because we see people as the problem. Yet people are not the problem, evil is the problem! But you can't fight evil with evil, you must fight evil with good (Romans 12:21). Choosing peace provides an atmosphere for good to thrive (1 Timothy 2:2-3).

Peacemaking is <u>not</u>; however, what most people perceive it to be! Peacemaking is <u>not</u> lazy, weak, cowardly or dumb. Peacemaking is <u>not</u> giving in, rolling over or playing dead. Peacemaking is <u>not</u> giving up what you want so someone else can have their way. Peacemakers do <u>not</u> surrender but fight to find a better way!

Peacemaking is the highest and best use of who you are and what you have. Peacemaking is a product of purpose, power and positivity. Peacemaking is <u>not</u> selfish (1 John 2:16) so what peacemakers do does not die with them. Peace is something everyone wants but Jesus exhorts His followers to actually make peace (Matthew 5:9). You see, it is not enough for you to have peace, God expects you to be a change agent, producing peace, not just for yourself, but for others as well. Instead of focusing on individually being the best, peacemakers focus on making everyone better. They understand that God works best in an atmosphere of peace. Peace is supreme and superior to war; peacemaking builds up and leaves everyone with more.

So, before the Devil can spoil another Christian or hinder another event (Proverbs 22:3), put peace into action and fulfill God's intent (Romans 14:17; 15:13 & Galatians 5:22). Go forth and reconcile. Go forth and mend. Go forth and heal. Go forth and cause violence to cease. Go forth God's chosen vessel, go forth and make peace!

PEACEMAKING:
Discussion Questions

Who does God expect to make peace?

What is the benefit of peacemaking?

When is peacemaking necessary?

Where in the scriptures is peacemaking extolled?

Why does peacemaking get ignored?

How can you be a better peacemaker?

III. ABIDING

A BELIEVER'S PRIMARY RESPONSIBILITY IS to grow spiritually (1 Peter 2:2; 2 Peter 3:18; 3 John 1:2). Spiritual growth; however, does not take place simply by deciding that you want to grow spiritually (John 1:10-13 & 2 Peter 1:21). Spiritual growth only takes place in an environment and a context that is rich with the presence of God's Spirit (Psalm 1, Ps. 92:13 and 2 Corinthians 3:6). In the Gospel of John Chapter 15 Jesus explains this concept. He says, "Abide in me, and I in you. As the branch cannot bear fruit of itself, except it abide in the vine; no more can ye, except ye abide in me. I am the vine, ye are the branches: He that abideth in me, and I in him, the same bringeth forth much fruit: for without me ye can do nothing" (John 15:4-5). In other words, we can want whatever we want BUT *without **Him***, we are just left wanting.

Being a mighty man or woman of God or being mightily used of God does not happen overnight. It is not instantaneous like being born again. Jesus uses the term "abide" over and over again to convey the truth that you must spend time with God. The word used in the original language was the Greek word "meno", which means to remain, stay, wait, endure, continue or last. It can also be translated "abode" which means a dwelling place. So Jesus is saying that if you want to be or do anything significant in the Kingdom of God you've got to live with Him. He must become your dwelling place!

Inasmuch as God's will and the believer's intention is to grow, it is the adversaries' will to hinder, hobble and halt any such growth (John 10:10)! The devil has everything in this world working to keep you from abiding! 1 John 2:14-16 says, "I have written unto you, fathers, because ye have known him that is from the beginning. I have written unto you, young men, because ye are strong, and the word of God abideth in you, and ye have overcome the wicked one.15 Love not the world, neither the things that are in the world. If any man love the world, the love of the Father is not in him.16 For all that is in the world, the lust of the flesh, and the lust of the eyes, and the pride of life, is not of the Father, but is of the world."

Don't be fooled by the seemingly innocent cares of the world! They are designed to choke the very life out of you (Mark 4:19-21)! The Devil is so sinister that He will use what seems to be good things to keep you from the best thing (Luke 10:38-42). He specializes in distractions, distortion, detours and doubts that lead to division and disconnection from the very thing you need most (Zechariah 3 & Revelation 12:10)! But you don't have to let it happen (Genesis 4:7, Matthew 16:18-19, Matthew 18:18, 2 Corinthians 10:4-6 & Ephesians 4:26-27)!

Every saint must endeavor to take control of their life back from the devil and envelop it in God (1 Samuel 30:8). We must entreat God to enable us to accomplish His will for our lives (Ephesians 3:20). We must choose to enter into the strait gate and dwell with God (Matthew 7:13 & Luke 13:24) and most importantly we must, **endure** as webster's dictionary says of abiding, to act in accordance with, to tolerate, bear and stand and to continue, persist and stay in Him that we might be all that He intends for us to be. This is the reason He sent our savior as Emmanuel, God with us, now is the time to choose to be with Him (Isaiah 26:3)!

ABIDING:
Discussion Questions:

Who is responsible for your spiritual growth?

What does spiritual growth look like?

When does spiritual growth take place?

Where do you have to be in order to be fruitful?

Why is being spiritually minded worth the effort?

How do you plan to abide at a greater level? What adjustments will you make in your daily life?

SCRIPTURE MEMORIZATION

You know the saying, "your body is here but your mind is somewhere else". To really be with someone... to really abide with them you've got to listen and internalize what they say. Only by really paying attention and considering what someone says can you get to know and appreciate who they are. This is never more crucial than when you can't see the person. I remember when I was deployed, I would write to my wife the most heartfelt letters. I would say things that I hoped would solidify our relationship and immortalize our love for one another. I would ask her whenever we spoke if she had received the letters that I sent. Had she received a letter and not read it by the time we talked I would be heartbroken and not really want to talk about anything else until she had, with complete concentration, read my letter and felt my heart through my words.

So, it is with God and the letter He has written to His Beloved. He wants you to cherish His words and take them to heart. He is undoubtedly heartbroken that you would have His Word in your possession and not take the time to read It. When His Word is read, do you hold it dear like the precious expression of goodwill and devotion it was intended to be? Do you hide it in your heart and think about it throughout the day (Joshua 1:8 & Psalm 119:11)? Do you consider what He has said and what He wants before you make decisions (Romans 12:2)? Or do you ignore this timeless treasure that was sent to uphold you and propel you into your purpose? What do you do with the Word of God (1 John 1:1)?

The mark of someone who really desires to grow in Christ is that they will abide in God's Word (John 8:31). Jesus said that if you love Him you will do what He says ("keep My commandments"- John 14:15). People mistakenly believe that the Word of God is sent to condemn them. They think because the Word calls them to repent, because the Word offers rebuke, because the Word provides correction and tells them the truth about the consequences of ignoring God; that the Word is against them. Nothing could be further from the truth. Just because the Word makes you feel bad initially because of the faults found in yourself, it doesn't mean that it is not for your good. Like any good friend, its purpose is to heal, set free and forgive. The Word does not condemn you but rather commands you to be free from sin! The light of God's Word is not your enemy. Rather the darkness of sin is what has already condemned and imprisoned you to a life far less than God's best (Hosea 4:6). But God sent His Word to save you! Read God's Word for discovery, to know who you are in Christ. Study God's Word for access, to grow in your inheritance in Christ. Memorize God's word for increased ability, to show forth God's glory... accomplishing what you were created to do (Daniel 11:32). After all, this is God's purpose in writing a love letter to you!

SCRIPTURE MEMORIZATION:
Discussion Questions

Who is the author of the Bible and to whom was it written (2 Peter 1:21; 1 Corinthians 10:11)?

What is the purpose of God's Word (Psalm 107:20)?

When do you invest time into God's Word (Luke 4:18)?

Where do you suppose you are in relation to where God wants you to be concerning His Word (Romans 12:3)?

Why is it important to take God's word to heart (Romans 10:8-9; Matthew 13:19; Mark 4:15 & Luke 8:15)?

How do you plan to memorize more of God's Word?

DAILY DEVOTION

JESUS TAUGHT US THAT whenever we pray, we are to ask for our <u>daily</u> bread (Matthew 6:11 & Luke 11:3). <u>Daily</u> bread speaks of the provision that we require from God as our Sustainer on a <u>daily</u> basis. This bread is not primarily material. The Bible says, "But he answered and said, It is written, Man shall not live by bread alone, but by every word that proceedeth out of the mouth of God." (Matthew 4:4). Jesus taught that we should not be consumed with material possessions but with the true treasure of heaven (John 6:26-35). Jesus is that treasure. Jesus is that bread. He expects us to seek from God our spiritual nourishment in Him on a <u>daily</u> basis.

There are things we do <u>every day</u> whether we feel like it or not. Everyone alive breathes <u>every day</u>. Most people eat <u>every day</u>, drink <u>every day</u> and make their body presentable ...<u>everyday</u>! If we do all of this for our physical well-being, is it odd, extreme, overbearing or unreasonable that God would want us to attend to our spiritual well-being on a <u>DAILY</u> basis?

Throughout the Bible there are expressions of religious devotion that are required of the adherents to be performed <u>DAILY</u>. One example is found in Numbers 28:24, "After this manner ye shall offer <u>daily</u>, throughout the seven days, the meat of the sacrifice made by fire, of a sweet savour unto the Lord: it shall be offered beside the continual burnt offering, and his drink offering." Another is found in Ezra 3:4 "They kept also the feast of tabernacles, as it is written, and offered the <u>daily</u> burnt offerings by number, according to the custom, as the duty of <u>every day</u> required;" Even after Jesus had ascended back to the Father, the Apostles taught the Early Church to seek God on a daily basis (Acts 2:46).

The Devil <u>does not</u> take a day off when it comes to orchestrating your downfall (Luke 4:13). So, you cannot take a day off in making sure you stay in grace and grow in God (1 Peter 5:8). The Devil wants to make your life as difficult as possible, especially when God starts to work in your life. One example of this is found in Exodus 5:13 where it says, "And the taskmasters hasted them, saying, Fulfil your works, your <u>daily</u> tasks, as when there was straw." The Egyptians already had the Hebrews in servitude but as soon as God began to move on their behalf the Egyptians made life harder for the Hebrews by taking away their straw and demanding the same production of bricks. The Bible conveys how persistently Delilah pressured Samson. In Judges 16:16 it says, "And it came to pass, when she pressed him <u>daily</u> with her words, and urged him, so that his soul was vexed unto death;" In the Psalms, David gets at the heart of the enemy's constant challenge when he says in Psalm 42:10 "As with a sword in my bones, mine enemies reproach me; while they say <u>daily</u> unto me, Where is thy God?" What a question, "Where is thy God?!" And He said that they said this to him on a daily basis! But when you've spent time with God and waited long enough to sense His presence, you can respond like David did saying, "The Lord is my light and my salvation; whom shall I fear? the Lord is the strength of my life; of whom shall I be afraid?" (Psalm 27:1)

You will never experience the full presence and blessing of the Lord until you get a strong desire to experience God personally, and that, on a daily basis. Jesus said, "Matthew 5:6, "Blessed are they which do hunger and thirst after righteousness: for they shall be filled." The ones who get filled are the ones who hunger and thirst. John 7:37 says, "In the last day, that great day of the feast, Jesus stood and cried, saying, If any man thirst, let him come unto me, and drink." The condition for getting what God has for you is hunger and thirst. Hunger and thirst represent longing, passion, desire and an acknowledged need that drives you to seek God!

<u>Daily devotion</u> is the answer to your soul's hunger (Psalm 42:1-2). It's the relief from your daily frustrations (1 Peter 5:6-7). It's rest from your hard labor. (Matthew 11:28). It's the peace that surpasses your circumstances (Philippians 4:7). It is the transformation you need in your life (2 Corinthians 3:18). It is because you walk in fellowship with the Father that you have the fuel you need to get further on your journey (1 John 1). Daily devotion simply makes you better!

God gives an open invitation (Isaiah 55:1-2) for you to get what you need in Him. Though so many ignore this invitation on a daily basis (Romans 10:21) God is faithful and stands at the door of your heart, waiting for you to answer the call (Revelation 3:20). Do you want to be made whole (John 5:6-14)? Do you want to experience the abundant life God has for you (John 10:10)? It's impossible to have it on your own... BUT with God you can! But you've got to seek Him (Hebrews 11:6). You've got to want Him. You've got to open your mouth wide and wait for Him to fill it (Psalm 81:10). When He does, you'll be glad that you did!

DAILY DEVOTION
Discussion Questions:

Who is responsible for the quality of your spiritual life?

What is necessary to grow in God?

When are you in fellowship with God?

Where do you purposely make a place for God?

Why do you personally think daily devotion is necessary?

How do you plan to increase the quality and quantity of your time with God?

ATTITUDE OF GRATITUDE

THANKSGIVING IS AN OFFERING (Leviticus 7:13-15 & Psalm 50:14)! This offering is commanded by God to be given at all times and in all situations (1 Thessalonians 5:18). This command is not mitigated by your circumstances nor do you have the right to pick and choose when to offer it (Ephesians 5:20). It is not always easy. It is not always convenient. But it is always commanded and always worth it!

"**H**ow can I offer thanks", you might ask, "when I feel my situation is anything but thankworthy?" The answer is that God's purpose, plan and promises are not determined by how you feel. Your feelings are so fleeting, so transient, so subject to change that no decision can justifiably be made based solely on how you feel. It would be a wrongful shame to deny God His due honor just because you don't feel like giving Him the glory!

Acknowledging God for who He is, despite what He has allowed in your life, is an act of faith and is often a sacrifice (Hebrews 13:15). Acknowledging God's goodness does not in any way minimize or negate legitimate human emotions like anger, hurt, grief, rejection, remorse or shame (Ecclesiastes 3:1-8). It in no way takes away your right to feel that way. But choosing to be grateful despite your circumstance does give you the benefit of a heavenly perspective. A heavenly perspective or "an attitude of gratitude" sheds light on your situation. It reminds the believer that their problems are temporary (1 Peter 5:10). As the saints of old said, "trouble doesn't last always" but our God is timeless and His reign is for all eternity and sooner or later He'll make all things right (Romans 8:18-28, Revelation 21:4 & Revelation 22:20)!

No matter how you feel, it is in your best interest to maintain an attitude of gratitude. This is not only because it widens your perspective in the midst of your problems but it also maintains your access when the adversary wants to cut you off (Psalm 100:4). Job demonstrated this when Satan attacked his family, fortune and fitness. Job did his best in the midst of his grief to keep his attitude right when he said, "Naked came I out of my mother's womb, and naked shall I return thither: the Lord gave, and the Lord hath taken away; blessed be the name of the Lord" (Job 1:21).

Knowing that the path of salvation is paved in suffering, the Holy Spirit, through Peter, admonishes us to choose to have the right attitude. 1 Peter 4:1-2 says, "Forasmuch then as Christ hath suffered for us in the flesh, arm yourselves likewise with the same mind: for he that hath suffered in the flesh hath ceased from sin; That he no longer should live the rest of his time in the flesh to the lusts of men, but to the will of God." Paul also writes in Philippians 2:5, "Let this mind be in you, which was also in Christ Jesus". We are never more like Jesus than when we have an attitude of gratitude that undergirds our obedience.

Salvation, you see, opens the door to all that God has for you in Christ (John 10:7-9). But it is your attitude that walks you in. Attitude is a weapon God gives us to wield. Without the proper attitude, you open yourself up for the enemy to steal. You will miss out on God's blessing and this battle you will lose if an attitude of gratitude you fail to choose (Ephesians 4:23).

ATTITUDE OF GRATITUDE
Discussion Questions:

Who is responsible for your attitude?

What is the basis for your current attitude?

When are we expected to offer thanksgiving?

Where does an attitude of gratitude get us?

Why is your attitude so important?

How do you plan to maintain your access to God?

LOCAL CHURCH PARTICIPATION

THE CHURCH (CALLED OUT ones) was established by God. It is the only legitimate vehicle ordained to bring about the Kingdom of God. The Church transcends governments, race, economics and education. Many people have a problem with the church. Let me rephrase that...many people have a problem with the people who participate in organized religion. Many people say that they love Jesus but have a hard time with the rules, rituals and religious people who regularly attend church. They will freely say, "I love Jesus but it's the church folk I have a problem with". Well, perhaps to their dismay, the Church was Jesus' idea (Matthew 16:18) and the church folk are His (John 10:28-29 & Ephesians 5:22-33). So really when you have a problem with the church you have a problem with Jesus (Acts 9:4).

Compassion is at the heart of God's relationship with us and it is the motive behind God's commands (2 Kings 13:23, 2 Chronicles 30:9, 2 Chronicles 36:15, Psalm 78:38, Psalm 145:8, Lamentations 3:22, Matthew 9:36; 14:14; 15:32; 18:27-33..). One reason God established the church, in addition to spreading the Gospel, was to show His people compassion. <u>God uses people to bless people</u>. God's expectation is that as people join His family by being born again and joining churches, the people in the church will love, nurture and walk through life with them- showing compassion (1 Peter 3:8, 1 John 3:17 & Jude 1:22). Compassion is sympathetic. It suffers or feels the same with another. "It is a feeling of deep sympathy and sorrow for another who is stricken by misfortune, accompanied by a strong desire to alleviate the suffering" (Dictionary.com). Do you want to grow in God's nature? Then showing and receiving compassion is part of the process and it is designed to be done most effectively in the home (family) and in God's house (church-a spiritual family) (1 Timothy 3:5 & 5:4).

Anointing is the outward manifestation of God's inward approval. Nothing is more anointed than unity. Psalm 133 describes the imagery of the blessing of unity. Verse 2 says, "It is like the precious ointment upon the head, that ran down upon the beard, even Aaron's beard: that went down to the skirts of his garments." On the other hand, it is hard to achieve unity when you can't even achieve assembly. Hebrews 10:25 warns us, "Not forsaking the assembling of ourselves together, as the manner of some is; but exhorting one another: and so much the more, as ye see the day approaching. Establishing the kingdom of God is a team sport. It works best when everyone is doing their part (1 Corinthians 5:4).

Requirements are placed on anyone that is part of anything. Sports teams have requirements for their teammates. Companies have requirements for their employees. Governments have requirements for their citizens. Even families have requirements of family members. Every organization needs its organs to be organized. God expects His people to gather regularly and for everyone to be in place (Genesis 3:9, Acts 2:42-46, Acts 5:42 & Hebrews 10:25). From the very beginning of the New Testament church there were churches planted in every community (Acts 14:23). Every church had leaders. Every church had organization. And everyone that was saved was expected to participate in the church (Romans 12, 1 Corinthians 12, Ephesians 4:11-16 & 1 Peter 4:10-11).

Equipment makes the difference in a job done well versus a job half done. The Bible says in Ephesians 4:11-16 that it is the responsibility of church leadership to equip the saints for the work of ministry. If you only attend church but do not actually participate in church, you will lack the very equipping that God has provided for you to be most effective. You will never reach your full potential trying to operate half equipped! You must not only be equipped but you must exercise your equipment. There's no safer, more encouraging place to operate in your gift than in your local church. But your participation is required for you to be equipped and exercised.

So, with so many reasons, so much encouragement and with such commands from God, how can anyone who wants to grow in God neglect church participation? You'll never get where God wants you to be until you go the way God wants you to go.

LOCAL CHURCH PARTICIPATION
Discussion Questions:

Whose responsibility is it to show compassion?

What is the difference between attendance and participation?

When should you participate in your local church?

Where else do you get to exercise your gift and be equipped outside of the local church?

Why should you participate in your local church? Give the reason that means the most to you.

How do you plan to be more engaged and effective in your local church?

IV. GIFT SHARING

GOD GIVES EVERYONE SOMETHING (Exodus 4:2, James 1:17 & Romans 12:3) and to the saints He gives much over (1 Timothy 6:17)! As a matter of fact, He saves His best gifts for believers (1 Samuel 2:30 & Ephesians 1:3)! When God gives, He gives intentionally, purposefully and with expectation (Isaiah 55:11 & Matthew 25:24-30). When God gives you a gift, He intends and expects for *His gift* to keep on giving (Gen 1:11; 8:22, 2 Cor 9:6, Gal 6:7).

Intentionally choosing to share what God has shared with you is what God expects of His children (2 Corinthians 9:7, 1 Corinthians 4:7 & Hebrews 13:16). The mark of a believer is their willingness to share (John 13:35, 1 Corinthian 13). The mark of a mature and growing believer is that they plan... intentionally... looking for and making opportunities to share what God has given them with others (Acts 4:32, Romans 1:13 & Ephesians 4:28).

Victorious Christian living does not exist without giving! Spiritually speaking, if you ain't giving you ain't living. What God gives you goes nowhere until you share (Luke 6:38). When you carefully read the letter to the Philippians you will discover that the scripture everyone loves to claim, "my God shall supply all your need according to his riches in glory by Christ Jesus" (Philippians 4:19) was only given to believers who were mature enough (*baby Christians don't share*) to share their goods for the furtherment of the Gospel (Phil 4:15).

Eventually, we will all stand before God and give an account for all we did and did not do with what He gave us (2 Corinthians 5:10, Matthew 25:24-30). We will all answer for whether we did what He commanded us or not (Matthew 5:42, 1 Timothy 6:1). And we will all have to explain why we did or did not share what He gave us with others. You may have little or you may have much but whatever you have, God expects you to share it (Luke 3:11; 16:11)!

GIFT SHARING
Discussion Questions:

Who is responsible for sharing what God has given you?

What has God given you (physically, materially, intellectually, emotionally, socially or spiritually) that you can share?

When do you share what God has given you or when do you plan to share?

Where is the best place for sharing what God has given you?

Why do you not share more of what God has given you (what hinders you)?

How do you plan to purposely increase your giving, sharing, sowing and reaping?

SHARING SPIRITUAL GIFTS

GOD CREATED YOU (GEN 1:27, Ecclesiastes 12:1 & Rev 4:11). God chose you (John 15:16 & Ephesians 1:4). God destined you for great things (Daniel 11:32, John 14:12 & Eph 2:10). The things God created, choose, and destined you for are far greater than you or what you have experienced thus far (Haggai 2:9, Job 8:7, 1 Cor 2:9 & Eph 3:20). Since what God created you to do is so beyond you, He equips you to do extraordinarily beyond what you could do by yourself (Eph 4:12). This equipping is what the Bible calls a spiritual gift.

In accomplishing the will of God, God does not leave it all to human resources and ingenuity. God intervenes supernaturally in the lives of believers. Through the Holy Spirit's distribution of spiritual gifts God supernaturally endows believers with knowledge, insight, strategy, approach, faith, compassion, communication and abilities that they could in no other way wield (1 Cor 12:1-11). These endowments or gifts are part and parcel of the powerful promise of God's Spirit (Luke 24:49 & Acts 1:4).

For all that spiritual gifts are worth, their worth plummets to zero if they are not shared. Sharing is the signature of love and love should always be the motivation for sharing (1 Corinthians 13). If you desire to edify or build someone else up your participation is required. The gift God hid in you to bless others cannot do what it was designed to do without you (1 Peter 4:8). God's gifts are meant to be shared. The only reason God gave you the gift was for you to share it (1 Corinthians 14:12).

To grow in God, you must put your gift to work. But growth in God will reach a stalemate until you learn to identify, develop and share your spiritual gift. 1 Peter 4:10 says, "As every man hath received the gift, <u>*even so minister the same one to another*</u>, as good stewards of the manifold grace of God". Whatever you do in God's Name and Spirit let it be done to the glory of God and benefit of others. Share your gift (Rom 12:6 Phil 2:3 & Jame 4:3)!

SHARING SPIRITUAL GIFTS
Discussion Questions:

Who are your spiritual gifts intended to bless?

What are you to do with the gifts God has given you?

When can you share your spiritual gift?

Where is a good place to begin sharing your gift?

Why have you not shared your gift more in the past?

How will you share your gift more today than yesterday?

TAKING ADVANTAGE OF WITNESSING OPPORTUNITIES

SHARING THE GOOD NEWS of Jesus Christ is the natural outflow of a life that's connected to God. The only reason that Christians don't share is that their cups aren't overflowing. When you spend time with God you get His heart. The heart of God is to save souls.

The Bible declares in John 3:16 "For God so loved the world, that he gave his only begotten Son, that whosoever believeth in him should not perish, but have everlasting life." God is so serious about saving souls that He exchanged the most precious commodity in all creation (1 Peter 1:18-20) to save your soul and the souls of everyone you know and love. That's the value God places on soul saving.

Soul saving is the will of God. 1 Timothy 2:4, speaking about God, says, "Who will have all men to be saved, and to come unto the knowledge of the truth." It is His will that all be saved and know the truth. Again, 2 Peter 3:9 confirms this when it says, "The Lord is not slack concerning his promise, as some men count slackness; but is longsuffering to us-ward, not willing that any should perish, but that all should come to repentance." The reason God is patient is to give people who are perishing an opportunity to be saved.

If the love of God dwells in you, you will love souls enough to make efforts to extend yourself to evangelize. Anyone can evangelize, even a babe in Christ can witness with their testimony. Evangelism is the express mission, main function and God ordained commission of the church as a whole (Matthew 28:16-20). And it is essential to individual spiritual growth.

Not only are we encouraged to make efforts to evangelize, we are commanded to commit time and energy into discipling others. Jesus commanded it as His final parting words. And why would you not want to share such good news? Why would you hold life and the ability to save someone from perishing in the palm of your hand and not rescue them? If you do not share

Christ someone you know will go to hell because of your hesitation, neglect and unwillingness to share. Shame on you if you don't share the Gospel! You will forever live with the knowledge that someone's in hell when you had the power to prevent it.

God made you the life-giving light bearer. He made you the soul saving salt. What else are you good for? What else are you here for? Don't be so focused on yourself and your problems that you neglect your purpose. Grow in God and grab someone else to grow with you!

TAKING ADVANTAGE OF WITNESSING OPPORTUNITIES
Discussion Questions:

Who do you have an opportunity to share the good news with now?

What can you do to make sure your testimony is well received?

When is the best time for you to witness (share the gospel)?

Where do you think you are in your spiritual growth?

Why do you not witness more?

How can you be more effective in your witnessing?

GIVING TIME, TALENTS AND TREASURE TO GOD

EVERY GOOD THING YOU ever got in your life came from God. The Bible says, "Every good gift and every perfect gift is from above, and cometh down from the Father of lights… (James 1:17) In fact, God gave you the very best He had to give. For God so loved the world, that He gave His only begotten Son, that whosoever believeth in him should not perish, but have everlasting life" (John 3:16).

Even the days of your life are in the hands of the Lord (Job 12:10). Every day He gifts you with new mercies (Lamentations 3:22-23). What you do with each day shows your level of gratitude and where your true treasure lies (Romans 12:1, 2 Corinthians 5:15 & Matthew 6:21). When you've done all that you do in a day is there anything that you can point to and say, "I did that for God"? If not, then all that you've been doing is in vain (1 Corinthians 3:13 & 15:58).

Any talent you have you received from the Lord (1 Corinthians 4:7). From every talent given God expects a return (Matthew 25:14-30). God's expectation is that you give Him no less than your best (Ecclesiastes 9:10 & Colossians 3:23). Your best ought to produce results (Mark 4:20). If you have talents that are unutilized or utilized but not for the Lord, then you are not fulfilling God's purpose for your life (Ephesians 2:10)!

We do well to remember that any treasure we have came from God. Deuteronomy 8:18 says, "But thou shalt remember the Lord thy God; for it is He that giveth thee power to get wealth, that He may establish His covenant which He swore unto thy fathers, as it is this day." We are but tenants leasing what God allows for a season (Mark 12:1-9). When the season is over we must all give an account of what we did with what the Master gave us (Romans 14:12 & 2 Corinthians 5:10).

Don't ever think for a moment that when you give of your time, treasure or talent that you've done God any favors. God is pleased with your giving, but

He doesn't need you to give. God wants you to benefit from giving the way He benefits from giving. But to do so you've got to give like God gives. If you can't give yourself to anything then God can't give anything to you (John 16:23)! Give your time, talent and treasure to the Lord! Trust Him with every gift and get ready to be astonished at what else He will trust you with!

GIVING TIME, TALENTS AND TREASURE TO GOD
Discussion Questions:

Who gave you your time, talents and treasure?

What does He want you to do with it?

When does God expect you to get busy using what He gave you?

Where is the best place to begin using what God gave you?

Why did God give you time, talents and treasure (see Ephesians 2:10)?

How can you yield a greater return on all God has invested in you?

SHOWING COMPASSION

LIFE CAN BE LONELY, difficult and painful! We all at some time or another need compassion. That's why God sets the lonely in families (Psalm 68:6) and commands us to show compassion to others (Zechariah 7:9). Human compassion is a remnant of the residue of the image of God (Gen. 1:27). But our compassion has its limits and is sometimes insufficient. Often we need the supernatural compassion that comes only from God. For God's love has no limits and His compassion never fails (Lam. 3:22).

Compassion comes from the Latin "compati" meaning "to suffer with". Compassion sees suffering and is provoked to alleviate it. Compassion is a chief characteristic of God. Over and over again we are reminded in scripture to rely upon, depend on and cast ourselves on the mercies of God (Psalm 100, 136). Even the place where God would meet His people was called the mercy seat (Exodus 25:22). God; however, delights in conveying His compassion to His children through His children. Jesus is the best example of this. Over and over again the Gospels tell us that Jesus had compassion on the people (Matthew 9:39, Mark 1:41 & Luke 7:13). Jesus said, speaking of God's nature, that when we see Him, we see God and His compassion is God's (John 14:7-9 & Mark 5:19). He also tells us that He is our example to do as He has done (John 13:15).

Child of God, you have the privilege and responsibility to show God's character through sharing compassion. God wants people to know Him in His grace and mercy (1 Timothy 2:4) but if His children don't show Him then the world will never know Him.

Compassion that is not shown is compassion that is not shared (James 2:16). Just feeling empathy, sympathy or pity is not showing compassion. God gave us our feelings to serve a function. Compassion should compel us to pour out of who we are into the needs of someone else. Compassion's current flows contrary to the world! Compassion's current comes from the river that flows from the throne of God (Rev. 22:1) and exceeds human limitations (Ephesians 3:20). Let compassion compel your action and remember the measure you mete out will be measured back to you (Matthew 7:2) and when you sow abundantly that's how you'll reap (2 Corinthians 9:6)!

SHOWING COMPASSION
Discussion Questions:

Whose responsibility is it to show compassion?

What is compassion?

When is it right to withhold compassion?

Where does the Bible say that we ought to be compassionate?

Why is compassion critical to the Christian experience?

How can you more effectively share compassion?

V. TRANSFORMATION

God hates sin and you should too (Proverbs 6:16). Like God, you should hate the effects sin has on you and all that God has created (Isaiah 59:2, Romans 6:23 & James 1:15). Yet in the midst of all the degradation that sin has caused, God loves you, even while you're a sinner (John 3:16 & Romans 5:8)! Though God loves you just as you are, He knows it's not good for you to stay as you are. God's plan and work in your life is to change you (Philippians 1:6). His goal for you is that you be transformed to be more like Him (Romans 8:29, 1 Peter 1:16, 2 Peter 1:4 & 1 John 3:2).

As a Christian, your spiritual transformation is commanded by God's Word. Romans 12:1-2 says, "I beseech you therefore, brethren, by the mercies of God, that ye present your bodies a living sacrifice, holy, acceptable unto God, which is your reasonable service.2 And be not conformed to this world: but be ye transformed by the renewing of your mind, that ye may prove what is that good, and acceptable, and perfect, will of God."

The Bible specifically says not to be conformed to this world but to rather be transformed (James 4:4). In this text, the Holy Spirit, through the Apostle Paul's letter is emphasizing the difference between conformation and transformation. Conformity is behavior in accordance with socially accepted conventions or standards. When you conform to the world's conventions and standards, you are agreeing with and submitting to obey the world (Romans 6:16). But God says that the world's ways are not His ways and that you cannot walk with Him if you do not agree with Him (Isaiah 55:8-9 & Amos 3:3). Transformation on the other hand is not adhering to an outward pattern set by some outside force but rather transformation is a metamorphosis, an outward manifestation of an inward change. So, God is offering an alternative to the ways of the world (Galatians 5:16). The world may have solutions to change your situation, but God alone is offering to change you from the inside out. We have the choice to conform to the world and stay basically the same or obey God and see what it is that He is transforming us into.

Your transformation proves what the will of God is for your life. This is accomplished by the renewing of your mind. Until you change your mind you cannot prove, manifest, and give evidence of what God's will is for your life. To experience something new in God you've got to acknowledge something new about God. You can't experience Him in a different way while seeing Him the same way!

The work of God in the life of a believer is one of transformation. God promised in the Old Testament that the day would come when He would give us a new heart and put His spirit in us (Ezekiel 11:19; 36:26). The Bible declares that when we are in Christ, we are new creatures (2 Corinthians 5:17). And as we behold Christ, God is changing us into His very image (2 Corinthians 3:18).

Your goals in life should align with God's goals for your life. God has set some glorious goals for you but they all hinge on your cooperation in transformation (1 Thessalonians 4:3 & 1 Corinthians 2:9). If transformation is commanded by God's Word, proves God's will and is what God is working in you, then what are you waiting on…let's get on with the business of transformation!

TRANSFORMATION
Discussion Questions:

Whose responsibility is it to discern the will of God for your life?

What can be done to prove God's will for your life?

When are we to begin becoming like Christ?

Where does transformation begin?

Why is it important not to be conformed to the world?

How can you cooperate with the transformation that God wants to bring about in your life?

FILLED AND LEAD BY THE SPIRIT

Ephesians 5:18 *And be not drunk with wine, wherein is excess; but **be filled with the Spirit**;*

SINCE WE WERE CREATED in the image of God and God is a triune being, we, too, are triune beings. We are spirit, soul (mind, will & emotions) and body. God is Spirit, He came in a body and He has a mind with a will and emotions. God feels and so we feel. We not only feel but we need to be filled. When we are filled it produces the feeling of fulfillment for which each of us yearns. The quest for the feeling of fulfillment is the driving force that leads us to either greatness or great disaster. Since the fall, we do not naturally do what is right. Although there's a residue of God in us, we have so much that's ungodly as well. So God's remedy to our "natural" tendency is to offer His help…and there's never any greater help than God Himself. So God in His love not only gave Himself in the form of the Lord Jesus but when Jesus ascended He gave Himself in a new way, a promised way, a way that transcends the limits of Jesus' bodily form- God gave us His Spirit (John 16:7). And it is with His Spirit that He commands us to be filled so that we can each experience fulfillment.

Pentecost presented an opportunity of unprecedented potential! It provided for the persistent presence of God in the lives of His people. Prior to Pentecost, the power and presence of the Lord God would come upon His people on occasion. Now, since that powerful day, God said that I will be within you (Ezekiel 36:26). The Bible says that the Spirit of God actually dwells in believers (1 Corinthians 3:16).

Indwelling is the term theologians use to speak of the resident abiding of the Holy Spirit within the believer. It means that God's Spirit dwells within. This means that He's always present. This means that as a child of God you are never alone. The believer in Christ has an ever-present help in the Holy Ghost! It is so important that we understand the glorious richness of what we have in Christ. Being in Christ, we've opened the door for Him to be in us. He is in us, not with us. Unlike the way He was with the disciples when He walked the dusty roads of Galilee, we have Him in a greater more intimate way. God abides within the believer.

Remembering this fact is of utmost importance. Without acknowledging this you limit the possibilities and restrict the potential God has for you. You must recognize God with you if you are to cooperate with the working of the Holy Spirit in you. It affects your decision making, it affects your self-perception, but most importantly it affects your God-perception and what you expect Him to do in your life. Your expectation is what you're looking for God to do. You will always miss what you're not looking for...

It is the Spirit of God that makes all the difference (Ezekiel 44:23). That's why we need to walk in the Spirit! "In the Spirit" means in God's will. When you are in the spirit you cannot fulfill the lust of the flesh. When you are in the Spirit you are at your best. When you are in the Spirit, the Devil can do you no harm. Where the Spirit is there is liberty. Where the spirit is, the captives are set free. The spirit makes broken things whole. The spirit brings renewal to your soul. What's impossible with man is possible with God...in the Spirit!

Truth be told, we are helpless to overcome the flesh, defeat the devil or do anything noteworthy or of any significance for the Lord without His Spirit (John 15:5). Pride resists the Spirit and the Spirit resists the proud. It's time to humble ourselves, know God's Word and get with it. We've only got so much time and to redeem it we need His spirit!

FILED WITH HIS SPIRIT
Discussion Questions

Who has the privilege of being filled with God's Spirit?

What does it mean to be filled with the Spirit?

When was the Spirit made available to be within us?

Where does the Holy Ghost dwell?

Why do we need the Spirit?

How do we receive the infilling and refilling of the Spirit? How can we receive more?

SHOWING LOVE: EDIFYING, ENCOURAGING THOUGHTS, WORDS AND DEEDS- SELF AND OTHERS

Ephesians 4:29 Let no corrupt communication proceed out of your mouth, but that which is good to the use of **edifying**, that it may **minister grace** unto the hearers.

EVERYTHING YOU THINK, EVERYTHING you say and everything you do has an effect on you and those around you (Matthew 12:36). What you think, say and do will either have a positive effect, bringing the blessing of God to bear on the situation, or it will have a negative effect, resembling the works of Satan more than anything that has to do with God (2 Corinthians 5:10). This is true for you and all those with whom you come into contact. That's why the Bible tells you to renew your mind (Romans 12:2) and think positive thoughts (Philippians 4:8). You are who you think you are (Proverbs 23:7)! And you deal with others the way you think about them (Matthew 5:27-29). That's why when God judges an individual, He does so according to what's in their heart (1 Samuel 16:7 & Hebrews 4:12). The most important factor, what makes all the difference in whether you fly or faint, all comes down to how you think (Isaiah 40:31).

The problem with stinking thinking is that it doesn't stay in your mind. Luke 6:45

What comes out of your mouth comes straight from your heart. And what comes out of your mouth has the power to either build up or tear down others. When it comes to your spiritual life and that of others, it is God's will that you be in the buildup business. Jesus' disciples got in big trouble when they wanted to tear down people. We tear down thoughts and imaginations that exalt themselves above the knowledge of God, but we've only been commissioned to build people up. We begin by building ourselves up-` confessing what God says and praying in the Spirit. Then we are commissioned to build up others. Tearing down comes in the form of expressing adverse assumptions, complaints, unconstructive criticism, cursing, cussing, doubt, defeat, and disaster. But building up comes in encouragement, consolation, exhortation, faith, hope and love.

The difference is life and death (Proverbs 18:21). Jesus said, "For by thy words thou shalt be justified, and by thy words thou shalt be condemned."(Matthew 12:7) Ecclesiastes 12:14 For God shall bring every work into judgment, with every secret thing, whether it be good, or whether it be evil. God has given us the creative license to create our own outcomes with the words of our mouths.

In addition to what you think and say God is concerned about what you actually do. Intentions are important but only what you do gets done. And what you do can be destructive and damaging or be encouraging, develop and edify. You may have heard the saying, "your life is a gift from God, what you do with it is your gift back to Him." God created you to do something! The first command was to be fruitful, and multiply, and replenish the earth, and subdue it" (Genesis 1:28). When God saved you, when you were born again it was for a reason. Ephesians 2:10 says, "For we are his workmanship, created in Christ Jesus unto good works, which God hath before ordained that we should walk in them." There is something you are supposed to do. Any time spent not doing what you were created to do or doing something else is wasteful and dangerous (1 Samuel 11:1 & 1 Chronicles 20:1)! Put another way, whenever you are doing what you're not supposed to do you're missing out on what you're supposed to do and others miss out on what you were meant to contribute (Ephesians 4:16). You have the choice...to be the blessing or the curse... what do you choose to do (Deuteronomy 30:19)?

SHOWING LOVE:
Discussion Questions

Who is responsible for how you treat others?

In what business should every believer be engaged?

When you see suffering what do you say?

Where does behavior begin?

Why is it important to make sure your words and actions match your intentions?

How do you intend to show someone love in a new way?

ENGAGE IN OPPORTUNITIES TO NURTURE SOMEONE'S SPIRITUAL GROWTH

*Matthew 28:19 Go ye therefore, **and teach** all nations, baptizing them in the name of the Father, and of the Son, and of the Holy Ghost:*

THE GREAT COMMISSION IS for the entire church. If you are not actively engaged in intentionally discipling someone you are not doing the one thing Jesus commanded us all to do. If all you are doing is reading your Bible, praying and going to church you're falling short of His command. He did not tell you to read, He assumed you would read saying, "have you not read" (Matthew 12:3-5). He did not tell you to pray. He assumed you would pray saying, "when you pray" (Matthew 6:5-6). He did not tell you to go to church. He assumed you would go to church saying, when you are assembled together and again do not forsake the assembling of yourselves (1 Corinthians 5:4 & Hebrews 10:25). But He did tell you to make disciples (Matthew 28:19-20 NIV, AMP). Not good moral people, not religious church goers but disciples. The mark of someone newly converted is that they make a good confession, testifying to what God has done in their lives. The mark of a mature believer however is that they disciple someone else making sure there's a harvest in God's vineyard. Let us do what God commands, not majoring in the minors. And let us not be those who by now should be teaching (discipling) but are in need of someone to teach (disciple) us (Hebrews 5:12). Let's disciple someone.

DISCIPLE SOMEONE:
Questions for Discussion

Who does God expect to make disciples?

What is a disciple and what is the key element in discipleship?

When does God expect you to begin making disciples?

Where should we go to make disciples?

Why is it so important to engage in opportunities to nurture someone's spiritual growth?

How are you going to disciple someone different?

TURNING NEGATIVES INTO POSITIVES

2 Corinthians 10:4-5 (For the weapons of our warfare are not carnal, but mighty through God to the pulling down of strong holds;) Casting down imaginations, and every high thing that exalteth itself against the knowledge of God, and bringing into captivity every thought to the obedience of Christ;

THE BIBLE SAYS THAT believers are children of God, children of the light (Ephesians 5:8). As children of the light we should aspire to be like our Father Who dwells in light. The Bible tells us to be imitators of God (Ephesians 5:1) As His children we should display characteristics that reflect the fact that He's our Father. There is perhaps no greater attribute of God, nowhere that He is more distinguished or more apparently God than His ability to turn something negative into something positive. He did it in the beginning, creating something out of nothing. He did it when He brought order out of chaos, life out of death, beauty for ashes and joy out of mourning. He'll do it again when He brings this world to an end and establishes a new heaven and a new earth. And He does it every day in the lives of His believers. Joseph attests to this fact when he says, "But as for you, ye thought evil against me; but God meant it unto good, to bring to pass, as it is this day, to save much people alive." (Genesis 50:20). God is a turnaround specialist! This is the power of the God who causes "all things *to* work together for good to them that love God, to them who are the called according to his purpose." (Romans 8:28) The children of God are to work the works of God and make it their mission to turn every evil, every wicked, every negative thing into something positive, for the good of people and the glory of our God (Romans 12:17 & 1 Peter 3:9).

This is the purpose of faith. To turn things around. To turn adversity into anointing. To turn barriers into springboards. To take criticism and turn it into something constructive. To turn the devices of the devil into opportunities for deliverance. To turn envy into equipping. To turn fear into faith. To take every groan from every hurt and transform it into the grace to help. That's what faith is for. What are you doing with yours?

TURNING NEGATIVES INTO POSITIVES
Questions for Discussion:

Whose responsibility is it to turn negatives into positives?

What does it take to turn a negative into a positive?

When is it a good time to turn a negative into a positive?

Where in your life are there areas you need to execute a turnaround?

Why do you think turning negatives into positives is foundational to spiritual growth?

How do you plan to turn something negative into something positive for someone else?

CONCLUSION

GOD IS A PLANNER. And like Him, God wants us to plan (Luke 14:28-32). Our planning does not have to compete with God's plans but can be complementary when we submit our plans to His. If our plans support His will, He will support our plans. Proverbs 16:3 says, "Commit thy works unto the Lord, and thy thoughts shall be established". God created us in such a way as to be collaborative with Him concerning His creation. In other words, God has a plan but supplies us with raw materials and a blueprint and "waits" to see how we customize it. In Genesis 2:19 the Bible says, "And out of the ground the Lord God formed every beast of the field, and every fowl of the air; and brought them unto Adam to see what he would call them: and whatsoever Adam called every living creature, that was the name thereof". Notice how God brought the animals to Adam, gave Adam the assignment of naming but whatever Adam named it God from that time forth referred to it just as Adam had called it. And so, it is with our lives. God has given us the gifts, talents and callings. He has allowed and brought forth various opportunities into our lives. Now He waits to see how we will name it, organize it and operate with it. He then will abide in accordance with whatever we have created. So, let's get to planning, let's organize our time and let's conduct ourselves in such a way as to make the most beautiful versions of ourselves that we can offer back to God. In Jesus' Name. Amen.

If you have completed the Spiritual Growth Plan, congratulations! You have done what few before you were able to accomplish. And in doing so, I know you can see and feel the difference. Your life, your experience and everything you encounter will never again be the same! You are forever changed! Now go forth in the confidence of your new creation. May your exercise and preparation cause you to excel and abound in every situation. And may God, in response to your faithfulness, bring to fulfillment every promise entitled to you as an overcomer. In Jesus' Name. Amen.

www.ingramcontent.com/pod-product-compliance
Lightning Source LLC
LaVergne TN
LVHW081453060526
838201LV00050BA/1788